COBBLESTONE

ENDLESS DAYS OF FREEDOM

Early Works of Angus Mackay, Chef, Poet, Traveler

3/8/2008

Thanks to the following for permission to use the graphic images
in these poems:
G.G. Mackay: Water; Summer; Spring; An Ancient Waterfall; Life;
Distant Fog
E.J. Anderson: Fire; Air; Skimming Stones Toward the Sun;
Over the Top; Ghost Stars; The Secret Garden
A.H. Anderson: The Lion and Elephant; Winter; Toy Town;
I Saw the Devil; Gates of Dusk; Endless Days of Freedom
Photographs for the following poems are from Angus' portfolio:
Earth; Cities Across the World; The City Takes Care of its Own;
The Mall; Mean Streets; Palm Trees at Sunset; Missed; Rainbow;
In Memoriam
Art work by ARM was used for: Rainbow and In Memoriam
Art work by EJA was used for: Fire, Air and Ghost Stars
Art work by AHA was used for: Lion and Elephant, Toy Town,
Over the Top, I Saw the Devil and Gates of Dusk
This is the second edition which varies from the previous edition
only with the addition of the poem, In Memoriam,
written for Angus' uncle Alasdair, a forward and contents page,
the poems remaining the same.

FORWARD

I was sitting at a table on the sidewalk outside a Paris bistro contemplating my future. I had spent the last two years studying graphic design at Manchester's City College, yet I'd never worked for a design company and the only way I knew how to earn a living was in the catering business in hotels and restaurants which I'd done off and on since leaving school in Edinburgh. I closed my eyes as the sun beat down from an azure sky, the taste of café crème lingering on my palette after my customary breakfast of coffee and croissant. The waiter bustled here and there with busy hands and purpose of mind, the sounds of the boulevard filtered through the air, in the distance a wandering musician strummed his guitar and pedestrians chattered as they strolled by: mais oui..qu'est ce que c'est..d'accord.. merde alors. I could hear familiar sounds coming from the bistro's interior, a clattering of pots and pans, the sizzling of olive oil; the aromas of garlic and basil filled the air. I felt a sudden rush of relief sweeping over me as I realized that I loved cooking and working in kitchens and would continue with this incredible life that varied so much from day to day. I'd been down and out before but I survived. I knew at that moment what the future held: I would learn everything I could about cooking and catering. On my return to Manchester, I enrolled in a catering course at the city College and continued to earn my daily bread in the pubs and clubs of that great metropolis.

(Revelation: from the journal of ARM)

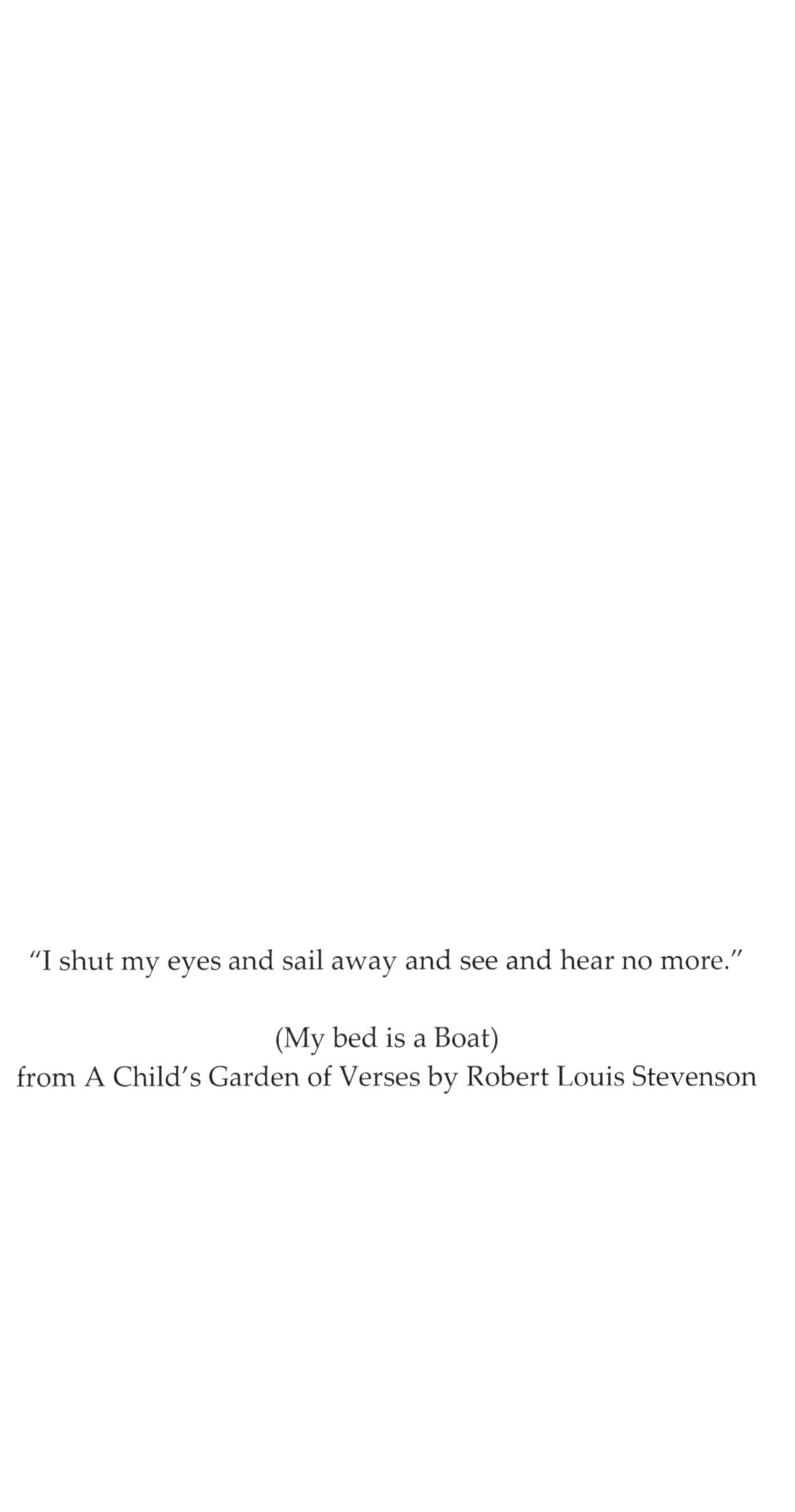

"I shut my eyes and sail away and see and hear no more."

(My bed is a Boat)
from A Child's Garden of Verses by Robert Louis Stevenson

CONTENTS

WATER
Silent water, life giver, diviners search
Divers search among sea wrecks
The sea so abundant in life
Water: calm, life giver, water in a storm
becomes life taker
The sea, moving home to shark, and whale
Water crashes on rocks, covers hi-ways
Breaker of bridges, rushing, give way
Ever hazardous becomes cool waterfall
running, bubbling
Love to hear its sound, river speeds to sea
Life giver, life taker, divine, precious, like life

FIRE

Pushing through the storm we cut over the
countryside
With time to steal, while we brace ourselves for
winter's jaws
Distant sun in the late afternoon's sky beckons us
to its light
A thousand nuclear storms with a smiling face
Fire, our first discovery rooted us in its necessity
Fire, our last image on a journey in search of light
We are still early man as we reach toward its
mysterious warmth
Sheer depth its mystery, as the journey spills deeper
Into the afternoon's dusk
Sun takes its leave too soon like a cabaret that must end
Evening's curtain brings his show down
Our journey continues, as still we search, still we move

SUMMER

A ship steers under a hot sun
A southern breeze blows upon the galleon
Somewhere on this undiscovered land
Cool palaces sit under the relentless sun
While gardeners pray for a storm
Sun beats down on the harbor front
Heat haze rises from the street like an
escaping bird from a cage
We hide from the sun where we can
Tender is the night as we sleep under a cool moon
That reflects on the still sea like an open window
My bed is cool and dreams reach out
To the northern breeze that blows thru the night
Cowering from the fire that is daylight

SPRING

Spring, the gryphon rising from the eternal
winter
The new land is rising in celebration
Leaving winter's burning city.
Below the trees its rivers break into song
Crashing over icy rocks like a thousand
wild horses
Buds grow under the tracks of the A-line
on the east side
The season's crops grow anew
This now fertile land under the rays of the new
rising sun
That breaks through, chasing winters shadows
away.
Migrant birds make their way home across
a new horizon
North wind blows across fields of wheat
This most fragile of seasons and bringer of dawn
From winter's last night

AIR

Drifting in the open sky, a balloon moves
Across the morning shadows, across the
distant light
Still it moves, floating across the land
Aimlessly, endlessly drifting thru the
day's light
That traverses over time, sky and air
Pushing this drifter toward the dusk.
Dusk's sky-air cooling in the sun's demise
Still it drifts, far from earth's grasp
A prisoner of the north, east, south and
west wind's tide
Evening's sun, cold air, another drifter
Far and beyond this land, still it continues
Together they go, through the days of light
The endless days of light

EARTH

The earth I walk on takes me on winding roads
Takes us on freeways as we pass airfields
We land on earth from the sky
We travel further, on asphalt, to cities around
the world
To ancient ruins in Greece, born of the ground
under a burning sun.
Fishermen in Sicily come ashore
From an open sea, on to earth at last
Boats bleached and worn under the sun
Bicycles weave among heavy traffic in Shanghai
Wobble on the road, on the way to work
Warriors in Kenya tend their livestock
On the open plains of this spacious earth
Wander among the miles.
Traffic moves, on a road in Paris, among the suburbs
To their destination, high speed and stop signs
It grinds to a halt on a Los Angeles southbound exit
On the earth, we move slowly
Natives travel in the highlands of Peru
Under a blue sky, shining upon the earth
Moving slowly from city to city around
Australia
In spaces we dream of
Dreamtime, aurora australialis, the hot plains
We travel the earth, our home, our space,
our language

AN ANCIENT WATERFALL

Cool water, soothing, moving, a never ending tale
Of mountain exits to highway, shaper of paths
Life giving force of nature's most ancient gift
Water covers, heals with its cousin's distant
sound of thunder
They shape the sand, pushing waves toward
a pulsing earth
Under the silent night stars, dawn's light
brings calm
Waves perched upon a cool home
Of sea horse, a lost city, schools, orcas
The deep sea becomes night for searchers
of wrecks
Discover a city, a lost city near Greece
Most ancient of civilizations, Crete and
ancient seafarers
The sea takes its toll and retreats, becomes
calm
Oceans, like night, mysterious and content
Still searching for our ancient city
It's within you and within me

LIFE

Life's creeping through the morning shadows
To raise the sleeping forms
The thrill of life is with them now
The crisp autumn air enhances our bodies
And we grasp at the shadows too

THE LION AND ELEPHANT
The house that haunts me still
Carries me and my dreams through the tangled
moonlit way
And into that garden of night
Where we lie deep in our images of a land
not far from here
Further we go over the endless miles
As if our journey were never to end
Our impossible dream continues
What is it worth to heal you in the night?
To spin you wisdom on fires of thought
Clothed by birds of the air
No more questions, in ancient morning
Of stripped stores and desolation streets
Sun cloud there is a time within every season
for fortune to visit
In knowledge we prosper, in dreams we capture
Season's winds which bring eternal spring
New day time to soar once again into the skies
She sleeps by my side: the form of an angel
A changing song, differing roads and impossible
boulevards
Separate heartbeats pray for a union of a soft fire
in the dusk
Pray for a life in the forest of the night
Clear as day you peered into my sleep
Where dreams run like yesterday's rivers
When I am cold, you keep the demons away
Where the backdrop of the memories begin
Of a time now gone, in dreams: they still march
Endless days under a blue forged sky
Where hope still lies, endless paths
Cut into the land and across the noiseless horizon

WINTER

In winter I listen from my window
To the sound of the highway
Traffic flows back and forth
I hear it cutting thru the icy night
North and south, exit left
Up above, the stars cast their dust
Deep into the winter night
Empty trees blow back and forth
Then hang down in solitude
An eerie silence in the cold air.
The north wind cuts across this frozen land
like a scythe
No yield to the plants that lie below
The clear, icy river moves with ferocity under
the moon's guiding light
Like a parent's caring hand.
Rain falls, nights are dark
We dream of spring, time will tell
The best time of them all

CITIES ACROSS THE WORLD
Into the open, across another state line
Out on the road again, another city, another
border line
Going from place to place as night falls
I see your face in cities across the world
Heading out over the crisscross of freeways
Soon day will become night in another time
Still I see your face as the sun falls once more
In cities across the world
Mountains change color in the rising sun's smile
Cold air all around as we enter another space
Greetings and new beginnings in this short time
Soon it's time to take off once more
Still as sleep captures me I see your face
The last image as the sun sets in cities
across the world

SKIMMING STONES TOWARD THE SUN

In the place of dwelling and dreams
We skim our stones toward the sun
I take the ghost train to the city of angels
Where time and stars collide
Watching the muse deliver her song
As the light of a new century's dawn
Reveals our footsteps in the sand
Each one in perfect isolation
Each one has shaped a new century

Sometimes when we look back
Remember a city built on seven hills
Swimming in time among the stars
As we skim our stones toward the sun

In dream time I see a garden of wonder
Where I wait for the muse to deliver her song
Until night chases us to morning
I threw myself asunder
Skimming stones toward the sun

THE CITY TAKES CARE OF ITS OWN
At night I run across the rooftops
Where the sky line embraces the sunset
Down below a city rushes by
As I run across these rooftops tonight
A helicopter snakes among the stars
The subway screeches into a tunnel
A shot rings out, then another
I keep thinking back to early days
When did this life on the streets claim me?
I hope what they say is true
The city takes care of its own
And this is no stairway to the stars
Just have to keep moving
It is a perfect night
And one to remember
On these rooftops tonight

TOY TOWN

Rag doll says goodnight
Cheeky moon sings sleep tight
The toys on the train
Cry hold on again
And the bear in the corner
Hidden from view, snoozes away
At the window, nearly new
Outside, the trees sway in the breeze
Soldiers inside mutter we better not freeze
Unlikely squeaks the wind-up doll
Ready to fall
Cat on the pillow purrs away
What does it matter
With their endless chatter?
It's okay for you chirps the bird on the curtain
You're getting fatter and far from the goose
Whispers the fox
With that a door locks
Bringing a sigh from the grandfather clock

THE MALL

I wonder where they are now
Sent out into splendorous gardens
Where the mist surrounds us
From the royal court to the green halls
No one knows the mystery that took them away
Whatever it was, great legends thus appeared

Now you have gone and left behind
So many memories and broken hearts
With an abundance of light
And youthful hope

I know the city outside with its blazing lights
Then I remember the silence
I can see the angels dance
In the transcendent light

Listen to the music until the last note
Every waking moment, listen to the last beat
To the last heartbeat, to the last bird singing
Everyone loses someone, sometime

I will always remember those crazy years
Those high adventures
But now, how can anything follow that?
This homeless prince sleeps alone tonight

MEAN STREETS

An angel must be with me on these mean streets tonight
As the sun disappears below these never ending freeways
Night's shadows creep under doorways
Like a demon's hiding form
Lurking under these towering buildings

As street lights shine down on these mean streets tonight
Every twist and turn, every reflection
In shut down dress windows and cold cut delis
Is a shape, unrecognizable, could be?..
No, just keep going onto fourth street and over to fifth

Gotta hustle now as I make my way on these mean streets
Someone suddenly brushes past with everything they own
I jump on a street car at last
We begin to move, twisting and turning
Bright lit streets are passing by
Rumbling high above the traffic now

As we turn onto my block
A taxi is rolling
There's a scream deep in the night
Lights are flashing
That street car is a long way off now
Maybe I was just lucky on these mean streets tonight

OVER THE TOP

When I was a soldier, it was over the top
Hunker down; listen for shells, gas attacks
When I was a soldier, no man's land was all we knew
Smoke all around, waiting for peace

A distant gun firing, another comrade has fallen
When I was a soldier, route march
We knew nothing, we were brave
How fitting for our King and Country

Gas masks, rations, when I was a soldier
We honor the fallen, and bury our own
Why we fight so young, we never get to know
When I was soldier, I went marching off to war
Hoping for one more day

PALM TREES AT SUNSET

The sun sets on another city left behind
Another northbound destination, another border
Sky high neon signs pass us by
East bound traffic heads to dreams and high hopes
Others go west on an empty promise
Rain begins to fall as the miles disappear
Darkness sets in and the freeway lights appear
Like angels pouring from a renaissance painting

It's another day, the roads below look like snakes
As they crisscross each other in a city not yet awake
The sky is blood red with silhouettes of palm trees
Sunrise casts its glow from east to west
We move ever on

I SAW THE DEVIL
The rain is falling
But from the windows of the great house
I saw him one winter's night
On and on he rode, back and forth
All was quiet from the kitchen
Though cruel blew the wind
Across the smiling moon
As it hung in the sky like an old china plate
Still he rode on and on
Down the lane into the distance
Casting a shadow across the horizon
In winter's glow
Until he was gone

DISTANT FOG

She stepped in like an old jazz tune
Her shadow shone through the rain
With the city skyline behind
Her beauty is the silken undertone
That makes my day
I wait on the corner
Just to watch her walk by

Where are we now?
The city's night has gone beyond
She is in my blood
Where is she now
The satyrs are gone?
And the city's evening's gone
Into the morning

She looks back on the rooftops at twilight
From a passing train
Where the city's sky has turned blood red
And a new star appears on the horizon

2 HOUR PARKING
8 A.M. to 5 P.M.

MISSED
I hear her footsteps in the sacred forest
She is my treasure swimming in dreams
Across the hills with three freeways
A figure emerges, remembering a life
Gone by, no ceremony, no goodbye
At night in dreams, endless knocking
Don't let the demons enter your door
We need light, no more unhappiness
Enter the dawn, I visited you
So much change no thought
The band played, the people cried
Banging of doors, almost haunting
The hour is up, give us an hour
A walk through the city, heart beating
Traffic passing by like phantoms
Among the walking dead
Pass under the freeway
Fear in places, don't look back
Dark night towards the end
Under a train tunnel, bright lights
Night of the dead, love thy city
She is my heartbeat
But where are you?
Now you are gone, leaving behind
So many memories, broken hearts
An abundance of light, youthful hope
I know the city outside with blazing lights
Clear as day you peered into my sleep
Where dreams run like yesterday's rivers
When I am cold you keep the demons away

"THE LIGHTNESS OF BEING"
Artist: Patrick T. McClain

GATES OF DUSK
I burn the candle, you shape the flower
I follow the eternal road where you begin
As we travel past the mountains
The train's shadows flicker and skip
Upon the golden trees in late afternoon gaze
Like a hare caught in a headlight
While running beyond a storm
What will we do now our king is gone?
Long since vacated our palace
It seems so empty now
Hardly a laugh echoes
Round this ancient gallery
So here's one for the revolutionary
Born beyond the storm
But now beyond the waves
I still see no one, nobody upon the shore
And so beyond the horizon
Life is missing its greatest artist
The space every compass searches for
And the sound, like waves that call our name

GHOST STARS
Night covers us with its robes of mystery
Like broken pieces of crystal
Hiding secrets that only the moon can see
From the deepest river to the distant lights of the city
Driving at night I see ghosts on the highway
Every shadow is someone new
Lights play tricks, ghosts are lights that move
Like reeds in the wind
Dancing to southern stars
The road is our king as we drive to western horizons
Into lights that guide us to the forbidden, the unknown
Regardless of time, driven by the procession
On our path to the eternal city

RAINBOW
Mixed blessings of a rainbow
The beat of angel's feet
Take me back to the place we met
Whispers in the dark nights
Weary for the light
Where is that moment in time?
We threw each other a line
In a metaphysical heartbeat
Wrap me inside your pain
Show me your smile
Standing in the shadows
Where great kings once stood
Great tears engulf us
Driving on the wrong freeway
I see you in the distance
The full moon bathes you in
light
I hear your voice in the dark
mountains
As clouds cover the forest
Like a bear claw
In dreams I capture you
In visions I see you
In the solace I hope
From the window I smell
The burning leaves
A childhood memory
remains
Like disappearing smoke
Then it is gone
As sleep comes to take me
on its journey
Your face appears and I
drift away

IN MEMORIAM

Goodbye to the town we knew as boys
Goodbye to the fields and meadows
Goodbye to the woods
Goodbye to the hills
And long winding roads in the dark
You had the touch, the magic touch
To reach into our hearts
You made us laugh, you made us cry
All with the stroke of a pen
Goodbye to the farms we worked all summer
Friends we made as we toiled
Goodbye to Sundays walking together
Carefree days indeed
You had the touch, the magic touch
To reach down to our soul
You made us laugh, you made us cry
All with a piece of charcoal
Remember when we walked those fields
And gazed at the Moorfoot Hills?
Remember the wee clay bottle
Buried in the soil?
A treasure trove of broken china
When we were rich inside.
You had the touch, the magic touch
To reach into our hearts
You made us laugh, you made us cry
All with the stroke of your pen.
Goodbye to the bridges
Goodbye to the art, painting, the lochs
The Scotland I love
Goodbye my friend, goodbye
We'll see you again someday

THE SECRET GARDEN

Where to Now?
We are left with a memory or two
A photograph, a smile
Somewhere along the line
A flickering image
Somewhere in Time

That was then, upon my return
Into your wishes we go
In our shadow we disappear
Into the secret garden
With our hearts we talk
What is written within.
Is this the promise we made?
Now is forever
What we have shall grow, and grow
In a place I cannot quite recall

Where are we now?
Are we still in time
Where we left off
Or do we move further on
Do we still search the sea?
Now I am tired, take me to the sacred place
Now I hear the music, take me to the garden

ENDLESS DAYS OF FREEDOM

From the bridge over the endless river
To the water's edge that hurried the mills
Ever turning the water that ran
As we come home in winter's dusk
Hurried by the smoke that bellows
From the great house on the horizon
Past the fields of half- forgotten trees
That stand like giant hands
In evening's unforgiving light.

Where the backdrop of memories begin
Of a time gone by, in dreams
Where they still march
Endless days under a blue forged sky
Where hope still lies and endless paths
Cut into noiseless horizons

On and on we go
Our endless journey is almost done
Although we are far and deep in winter
In our endless days of freedom
Our endless days of innocence
We are home and just as we close the door
We listen and we hear
The sound of the last train

We listen until we can hear it no more
And in the silence
The endless day has slipped beneath us.

Epilogue

The idea of foreign climes has always appealed throughout history. My first record of migration was of my great, great, grandfather coming from Wick to Edinburgh seeking work as a shoemaker. A few years later around the turn of the century he headed to Canada following in the footsteps of fellow Scots looking for a better life, however he returned home after 9 months due to the unbearable weather and a diet of herring every day. The next family member to go abroad was my great uncle, a singer of Scots songs who toured Canada and America but died aboard the Lusitania on the return voyage from New York in 1915. I also had a great uncle and aunt who lived in China in the 1920s as missionaries for about 30 years. My great, grandfather did a tour in the great war and fell at the Battle of the Somme in 1916. My grandmother lived in France in the 1930s after getting engaged but had to return home at the outbreak of world war two. Migration continued with my grandfather who moved to Africa in the 1960s partly for health reasons but returned to settle in Devon. My uncle Alasdair talked fondly of a visit he made to Los Angeles in the 1970s and he made it sound like a magical place: my god Disneyland! Other memories of far-off places come to mind when I recall our friends from Australia who turned up on our doorstep when I was about 9 or 10 years old and stayed for several months but eventually decided that after all they would prefer to live Down-Under. Around this time, we were corresponding with my aunt and uncle in Queensland by tape messages; they were probably telling us how nice the weather was while we would reply with how miserable our weather was and thanks for telling us what a nice time you are having. The theme of migration continues when my uncle Robert who was a bee farmer in Somerset married a lady from South America and moved to Colombia to take up ranching on the family farm. They later emigrated to Vancouver Island. While this was happening, my father was working in Saudi Arabia and making plans to set up business in California, which brings us nicely to the theme and subject of my story which concerns my travels from Scotland to California and my search for bliss as a poet.

(Just an immigrant: from the journal of ARM)

AFTERWORD
Observations of an immigrant in California
The clowns are out- The eternal Saturday night- It's dusk already- Immigrant
life on the mean streets of a frightened city- I found a quarter in the gutter-
There's opportunity on every corner – There's a vagabond standing in a
doorway with everything he owns at his feet-Dancing with the phantom- The
spirit of Ellis Island for all those who came through that immigrant line.

AFTERWORD
We cannot stop the freight train, It was always coming, but there is no turning, We didn't see it, And we couldn't hear it. Life is like a freight train, But when we are gone It still goes on and on.

PRAISE FOR THE AUTHOR

Adieu dear amiable youth! Your heart can ne'er be wanting! May prudence, fortitude, and truth, Erect your brow undaunting! In ploughman's phrase: God end you speed, Still daily to grow wiser; And may ye better reck the rede, Than ever did the advisor.
(Jim Lawrence quoting Robert Burns)

(2)

see your enigmatic smile, and in these words you left behind, casual notes in a little black book, somehow they ease the pain, they touch me deep inside. You are part of me, I am part of you, you are no more in time and place, but I feel you in the redwood trees, swaying in the warm breeze, around the world. You drift in and out of places from the past and places from the future too. You are everywhere you have been and everywhere you would be, moving on like the breeze, beside me in the redwood grove. I hear your voice sighing in the branches: Grieve no more nor talk of me with tears but laugh and speak to me as if I were beside you. When will we realize how alike we are to the trees, how it's good to be born?
(James Bruce)

ACKNOWLEDGEMENT

To Music Man, who prefers to remain anonymous: thanks for being a friend, for your inspirational music, your words of wisdom and your support through difficult times. I have enjoyed our talks, your art, and your clear vision. How many Bay Area restaurants have we had stopped at for lunch? I cannot count the ways, but it is dozens over the years.

Graeme Mackay (editor)

ABOUT THE AUTHOR

I was born in 1967 in Edinburgh, Scotland then moved to Midlothian at two years old where I spent the following seven years in the rural setting of Arniston Estate surrounded by open fields and tree-lined country lanes. I never took education seriously until 1989 when I enrolled in a graphic design course in Manchester whilst working in the local restaurants and pubs. Subsequently I enrolled in a culinary arts program and spent the summer holidays traveling to California, France, Italy and Australia. During this period, I developed the habit of keeping a journal with notes, poems and stories. Eventually I emigrated to California to work in the restaurants and hotels of the Bay Area

A FINAL AFTERWORD
Homeless Bees

I read the news today, it's true, About a million bees in San Joaquin, And though the news was rather blue, They had to pay the price without a queen, They lost there hives in a freeway crash, And though the bees were still alive, I don't know why, don't ask, But homeless bees cannot survive. A crowd of people stood under the trees, Nobody was really sure If they should stay, They'd never seen so many bees. Having cried all my tears yesterday, I could only stand and stare, Thinking life is a short affair.